Unbreakable

D1493825

What the Son of God said
about the word of God

Unbreakable

Andrew Wilson

Series Editor: Michael Reeves

First published in Great Britain in 2014

British Library Cataloguing in Publication Data
A record for this book is available from the British Library

ISBN: 978-1-909611-86-3

Designed and typeset by Pete Barnsley (CreativeHoot.com)

Printed in Denmark by Nørhaven

10Publishing, a division of 10ofthose.com
Unit C, Tomlinson Road, Leyland, PR25 2DY, England

Email: info@10ofthose.com
Website: www.10ofthose.com

1 3 5 6 10 8 6 4 2

Contents

Introduction: Where Do We Start? 1

And God Said: 5
The Story Of Scripture

1. **The Art of War:** 9
   The Authority Of Scripture

2. **True Like Jazz:** 13
   The Inspiration Of Scripture

3. **Dodging the Rocks:** 17
   The Unbreakability Of Scripture

4. **One Bride for Seven Brothers:** 21
   The Coherence Of Scripture

5. **It's Not About You:** 25
   The Centre Of Scripture

6. **Red and Black:** 31
    The Canon Of Scripture

7. **The Ship Is Made for the Ocean:** 37
    The Fulfilment Of Scripture

8. **You Can Always Trust the Light:** 41
    The Clarity Of Scripture

9. **Judgment, Miracles, Sex and Stuff:** 47
    The Challenges Of Scripture

10. **Oh No, They Won't:** 53
    The Sufficiency Of Scripture

11. **Restless Idol-Factories:** 57
    The Danger Of Scripture

Epilogue: 61
    The Interpretation Of Scripture

Further Reading 65

Notes 67

This short book is a perfect combination: one of my favourite writers, with brilliant thinking and a breezy style, tackles one of the most important issues you could ever consider. The argument is simple yet profound: when it comes to the doctrine of Scripture, we cannot go wrong if we hold to the perspective of Jesus.

Justin Taylor,
Senior Vice President at Crossway
and blogger at *Between Two Worlds*

Introduction:

WHERE DO WE START?

Books and talks on the Bible, in general, start from one of three places.

Some begin with the questions and problems people have with the Scriptures, and go through them one by one, explaining how best to think about them. I get that. The Bible contains puzzling details (swapping sandals in the middle of a love story), and upsetting stories (destroying Canaanite cities), and dramatic miracles (parting the Red Sea, really?), and factual difficulties (how did Judas die, again?), and unpopular teachings (sex is only meant for one man and one woman in marriage), and a confusing canon (what on earth is the apocrypha, and why don't we read it?), and so on. Therefore most of us have questions about the Bible – big, difficult, sticky questions – and engaging carefully with them is very important. But if we start from there, we risk putting ourselves immediately on the defensive and implying that our questions (which are different, as it happens, from the questions many cultures have asked) are the most important thing on the table. The chances are they're not. So that's not where this book begins.

Others begin with what the Bible says about the Bible. As circular as that might sound, it's actually quite sensible, because all sets of beliefs have to start somewhere; you trust reason because it's rational, you trust experience because it fits with your experience, you trust the Bible because it's biblical, and so on. Personally, though, I don't tend to do that, mainly because it looks suspiciously random (as in, why didn't we start with the Qur'an as our ultimate authority, or the Bhagavad Gita, or for that matter the *Daily Mail*?). So that's not where this book will start, either.

Instead, this book will use Jesus as the starting point. (That's controversial, I know.) Ultimately, you see, our trust in the Bible stems from our trust in Jesus Christ: the man who is God, the King of the world, the crucified, risen and exalted rescuer.[1] I don't trust in Jesus because I trust the Bible; I trust the Bible because I trust in Jesus. I love him, and I've decided to follow him, so if he talks and acts as if the Bible is trustworthy, authoritative, good, helpful and powerful, I will too ... even if some of my questions remain unanswered, or my answers remain unpopular.[2]

Don't worry: we'll get to some of the big questions, and the witness of the rest of the Bible, as we go. But we begin where the gospel does, and where Christianity does. We begin with Jesus.

And God Said:

THE STORY OF SCRIPTURE

You could summarise the biblical story like this.

In the beginning, God.

Everything was shapeless, and empty, and dark. Blobs of unsorted, unformed matter drifting through space. An enormous cosmic splodge. A scribble.

And God said, 'Lights.' And it happened.

And God said, and it happened. And God said, and it happened. And God said, and the earth did. And God said, and the animals did.

And God said, 'Go, have sex, have children, explore, rule, guard, keep. Have the run of the place. Watch out for one thing – that particular tree brings knowledge of good and evil, and you don't want a piece of that –

5

but otherwise, it's all yours. Enjoy.' And the humans did.

And the snake said, 'Did God really say that? Are you going to let your lives be restricted by what you think he said?' And the humans didn't. And it all went wrong.

And God said, and it happened.

And God said, and Abraham did. And God said, and it happened. And God said, and Israel didn't, although sometimes they did, but mostly they didn't. And God said, and it happened.

And God said, 'Here's my boy. I love him. Listen.'

And the snake said, 'Are you really the Son of God? Why not do this, then?'

And Jesus said, 'It is written.'

And the snake said, 'Well, what about this, over here?'

And Jesus said, 'It is written.'

And the snake said, 'Or this?'

And Jesus said, 'It is written.'

And the humans said, 'Who do you think you are? What are you playing at? Nobody can do that, except God. If you go there, you'll be killed. Are you mad? Are you demonised? He's blaspheming! No, Master, this will never happen to you.' And stuff like that.

And Jesus said, 'It is written in the Scriptures.'

And the snake said, 'Give it up, Miracle Boy.'

And Jesus said, 'How else will the Scriptures be fulfilled?'

And the humans said, 'Crucify him.' And it happened.

Silence.

And the humans waited.

And so did the angels.

And so did creation.

And so did the snake.

'Did God really say?'

Silence.

And God said, 'Lights.'

And it happened.

The Art of War:

THE AUTHORITY OF SCRIPTURE

That was the story in outline. We now need to go into it, a bit deeper.

At the start of the story, humanity is formed, then blessed, then sent, and then immediately tested. The snake, as we've just seen, goes straight for the issue of authority: 'Did God really say...?'[3] *Um. Ah. Well, you see, it's ... Come to think of it, he ... No, perhaps he didn't. And it does look juicy, doesn't it?* Crunch.

From now on, God says to the snake, there will be warfare between your seed and the woman's. You'll damage his heel, but he'll damage your head. One day a 'seed' will come, born of woman, who will resist your temptations, stand firm in the face of trials, and crush you and all you stand for. Crunch.

As the Old Testament continues, we get increasing clarity about who this 'seed', this snake-cruncher, is going to be. He's descended from Abraham, via Isaac, via Jacob, from the tribe of Judah, in the line of David, born of a virgin, in Bethlehem …

As the story reaches its climax the seed is formed (in Mary), then blessed (at his baptism), then sent (into the wilderness), and then immediately tested.[4] The snake is confident, seeing as Jesus hasn't eaten for six weeks: 'If you're the Son of God, command these stones to turn to bread.' But Jesus is ready. 'It is written,' he says, 'man doesn't live on just bread rolls, but on the words of God.' Crunch.

If you're going to quote the Bible to me, thinks the snake, *then two can play at that game*. 'If you're the Son of God, prove it. The Bible says that God will protect his chosen one – so jump off the temple, and watch the angels swoop in to catch you.' But again, Jesus is ready. He knows Psalm 91 inside out, and he knows it doesn't mean *that*. 'It is also written: don't test God.' Crunch.

The snake's final roll of the dice, then: 'I'll give you the kingdom, but without the suffering, if you just worship me.' Jesus doesn't hesitate. 'It is written: only worship the Lord your God.' Crunch. Game, set and match.

It's a great story, and there's a huge amount we can learn from it, but for now, just consider the way Jesus fights. He has the resources of heaven available, yet he fights by using the authority of the Scriptures. Not as a one-off, or as a change of tactics, but each and every time. 'It is *written* ... it is *written* ... it is *written*' he repeatedly emphasises. His position is unequivocal: 'You're trying to tempt me, but the Scriptures have spoken. That's the end of the conversation.'

Not only that, but each skirmish reveals a different aspect of Jesus' commitment to Scripture. In the first exchange, he shows that God's word is *enough*: whether you're wandering in the wilderness for forty days or forty years, you'll find that bread alone doesn't satisfy, but only the words that come from God's mouth.

In the second, faced with an attempt to distort the text's meaning, he shows that God's word is *coherent*: yes, Psalm 91 says that God protects his people, but Deuteronomy[5] tells us not to test God, and we need to hold those two things together (which certainly does *not* involve jumping off a building just to show off).

In the third, he shows that God's word is *authoritative*: if God tells us to do something, then we do it, no matter what anyone says.

Jesus, it seems, loved the word of God with his heart (being satisfied by it), his mind (understanding it), and his will (obeying it). If that was true of Jesus, I really want it to be true of me.

2

True Like Jazz:

THE INSPIRATION OF SCRIPTURE

Some journalists have a reputation for asking extremely tough questions. In the last ten years or so, men like John Humphrys, Martin Bashir and Jeremy Paxman have made careers out of putting awkward questions to powerful people in interviews, sometimes reducing them to silence. Nobody in history, though, asked tougher questions than Jesus. If he decided to cross-examine you in an interview, you were in trouble.

It's a Tuesday afternoon, and Jesus is surrounded by a group of Pharisees.[6] 'Whose son do you guys think the Messiah is?' he asks.

They know the answer to that one. 'David's.'

'But David, speaking by the Spirit, calls him "Lord", doesn't he? So how can he be his son?'

Silence. End of interview.

It's a brilliant argument. If the Messiah is nothing more than the 'son' of David – a distant descendant – then David wouldn't call him 'lord' or 'master', would he? That's not how we tend to talk about our great-great-great-grandchildren. But here we have David, speaking by the Spirit, referring to the Messiah as his lord. So he must be more than a descendant. He must be, somehow, greater than David himself.

Here we have David, speaking by the Spirit

Notice how Jesus refers to the author of the Psalm, though: *'David, speaking by the Spirit.'* This, more clearly than anywhere else in the historical records we have, shows how Jesus understands the inspiration of Scripture: the relationship between divine and human activity in the writing of the text. It's not *invention*, as if it were a question of 'David, speaking from his own experience', or 'David, speaking in line with the way he viewed God at the time'. Nor, on the other hand, is it *dictation*: 'God, proclaiming Hebrew words which David slavishly copied down', or 'God, writing words in the sky by the Spirit'. Rather, we have the divine and the human working together: *'David, speaking by the Spirit.'* It's *inspiration*.

Consider a jazz musician who can play all sorts of different instruments. Nobody, listening to Louis Armstrong, would ask whether the music was being made by Louis or his trumpet; everybody knows that the breath and the tune come from Louis, but the instrument through which the breath passes, in order to become audible, is the trumpet. The Bible writers, if you like, are the instruments of revelation – a trumpet here, an oboe there, a saxophone here – and they all make different sounds. But the musician, the skilled artist who fills them all with his breath and ensures the tune is played correctly, is the Holy Spirit. That's kind of how inspiration works.

One person who watched the brief interview with the Pharisees that Tuesday afternoon was Simon Peter. He later described biblical inspiration this way: 'For prophecy never had its origins in the human will, but prophets, though human, spoke from God as they were carried along by the Holy Spirit.'[7] Paul, who had trained as a Pharisee himself, agreed: 'All Scripture is God-breathed.'[8] (It may or may not be significant that both men wrote these things at the ends of their lives; older saints are often the ones who most insist on the inspiration of the Bible.) In saying these things, they were also reflecting the way the prophets themselves saw what they were doing: 'The word of the Lord came to ...', or simply, 'and God said ...' 'We aren't making this up,' they insisted. 'This is being carried along and animated by someone else.'

Scripture, like jazz, always is.

3

Dodging the Rocks:

THE UNBREAKABILITY OF SCRIPTURE

Everybody knows that Jesus was killed. What many people don't know is that, before they eventually succeeded, there were first several failed attempts to kill him.

It's winter, and Jesus is in Jerusalem.[9] He keeps saying provocative things: things which only Israel's God could truly say, like, 'I'm the light of the world', and 'I'm the bread of life', and 'I'm the good shepherd', and even 'Before Abraham was, I am.' One day, the Judeans gather round, like journalists swarming around a politician in trouble, and push him for a straight answer – so he gives them one. 'I and the Father are one,' he says.

That's blasphemy, they think. Quickly, they reach down for stones to throw at him: bits of rock, cobbles off the street, whatever is available. 'Not because of the works you've been doing,' they say – although they don't like those either – 'but because you, a mere man, are claiming to be God, you have to die.'

But Jesus is ready for them. 'Have you read your Bibles recently? Psalm 82:6, for instance? If the Scriptures call kings "gods" – and the Scriptures are the word of God, and they are unbreakable – then what are you getting so hot and bothered about? In a nutshell: if you're saying I'm wrong, then you're saying the Bible is wrong. But the Bible is *unbreakable*, right? It's the word of *God*.[10] So you should probably back off.'

But Jesus is ready for them. 'Have you read your Bibles recently?'

It's not just a clever line, plucked out of nowhere to win an argument. Right at the start of his teaching ministry, Jesus made it clear that he hadn't come to 'break to pieces' (or 'abolish') the Law, and that anyone who 'broke' it would be called least in the kingdom.[11] The unbreakability of Scripture is foundational, both for Jesus and for the Judeans he's talking to: since God has spoken through Scripture, then any argument that leads to the conclusion that Scripture is broken in some way, no matter how convincing it sounds, must be wrong. End of story.

That's hugely challenging. Many of us, when faced with a biblical difficulty – and there are plenty of those! – conclude that the Scriptures are broken. Maybe this didn't really happen. Maybe God didn't really say that. Hardly a day goes past without some Christian, somewhere, apologising for something the Bible says, and muttering something about it being a human book, complete with muddles and mistakes.

But if the Scriptures are the unbreakable word of God, as Jesus seems to have thought they were, then a different approach is needed. Maybe it's my interpretation, or my assumptions, that need challenging. Maybe there is something I don't know. Maybe the answer is in there, and I just need to look a bit harder.

Maybe I'm the one who is broken, rather than the Bible.

4

One Bride for Seven Brothers:

THE COHERENCE OF SCRIPTURE

'Teacher,' someone asked Jesus, 'you believe in the resurrection, don't you?'[12]

'Yes.'

'Well, there's something that's always bothered me about that. Moses says that if my brother dies and his wife has no children, I should marry her. But what if I'm one of seven brothers, and all of us marry her and then die without children? If the resurrection is real, that will mean she'll have seven husbands to choose from, right? But that's ridiculous. So the resurrection can't be real, can it? Na na, na na na.' And then they all did a little dance.

It might seem odd, in a serious debate, to make up a silly hypothetical scenario, and then act like you've debunked a crucial doctrine. (Lucky nobody does that today, isn't it?) It might look like a bit of childish game-playing. But it's actually quite a clever tactic. Not only is it an attack on the idea of the resurrection, but it's also an attack on the coherence of Scripture.

The Sadducees, one of whom asks the question, didn't just deny the resurrection; they also taught that although the Law was divinely given, the rest of the Hebrew Bible (the Prophets and the Writings) was not. So from their point of view, if something wasn't taught in the Law, then it wasn't true. The resurrection was a good example: yes, it was taught in the Prophets, but it wasn't taught in the Law, and some of Moses's instructions (like the one about marrying your brother's wife) made it look like a lot of nonsense. The Law, in other words, contradicts the rest of the Scriptures. Hence the little dance.

But, Jesus explains, as if talking to a small child, 'The reason you're wrong is that you don't know the Scriptures, and you don't know God's power. For a start, the resurrection doesn't involve marriage relationships anyway. But more importantly, the Law tells exactly the same story as the Prophets and the Writings on this one. If you would only read the Law properly, you'd see that the burning bush story reveals a God of the living, not of the dead.[13] You've got it all wrong.

'*You don't know the Scriptures.* You've read God's word so clumsily, and so superficially, that you haven't noticed how coherent it is: how themes can appear in Genesis and then wait until Isaiah before they're developed, and how doctrines like resurrection are hinted at in Exodus, even if they're not stated fully until Daniel. So you play off one part against another, without recognising that they're all given by the same God. If you understood the coherence of Scripture, the beautiful way in which it all hangs together, you would never make such a silly argument. But you don't, so you do.'

> '**You've read God's word so clumsily, and so superficially, that you haven't noticed how coherent it is ...**'

It's probably worth saying here that there's nothing wrong with being puzzled by the Bible, and asking how we should read this bit in the light of that bit. Sometimes, biblical texts are intended to be held in tension with each other, to make us think about them carefully.[14] Sometimes we may have to hold our hands up and admit: we don't know.[15] Sometimes a bit of imagination is required, to fit together accounts which differ in the details.[16] Many important ideas are not taught clearly until a fair way through the story – we call that *progressive revelation* – including resurrection, the Trinity, the priesthood of Christ, and so on. But the later bits don't contradict the earlier bits, any more than the fourth floor of a house contradicts the foundation it's built on. Scripture, when you get to know it properly and think about it carefully, is coherent.

5

It's Not About You:

THE CENTRE OF SCRIPTURE

If I had just been resurrected from the dead, and I wanted to show my friends and followers that I was alive again, I know how I'd do it. A flash of light, a trumpet fanfare, a loud *bang*, and then I'd suddenly appear in front of them – no, even better, above them – announcing 'It's me' in a booming voice as triumphantly as I could.

What I wouldn't do, I can be certain, is sidle up to them one day as they're walking home in misery, tell them off, take them through a detailed Bible study, tear a loaf of bread in half, and then vanish into thin air in the middle of dinner. Yet that's what Jesus did.[17]

The reason he revealed himself like this, it seems, is that he wanted to take them through the Scriptures, and show them how Israel's entire story points to him. Appearing with a bang would be impressive, but it wouldn't help them see how the centre of Scripture is Jesus himself. So after a quick rebuke – 'You guys really don't get it, do you?' – he goes through the whole Bible, beginning with Moses, and explains how all of it points to the suffering and glory of the Messiah. Apparently, knowing that Jesus was alive could wait. Knowing that Jesus was the centre of Scripture could not.

The difference in the lives of these two disciples was dramatic: 'Hey, didn't it feel like your heart was *on fire*, as he went through the Scriptures?' Later that day, when Jesus did a similar study with his other followers, Luke tells us that he 'opened their minds' as to what the Bible was about. That's the dramatic difference it makes, when you grasp that Jesus is the centre of Scripture. If you read the Bible as if it's mainly about Israel, or mainly about you, it's like reading it with a cold heart and your eyes shut. When you discover it's mainly about Jesus, and God's purpose for the nations through him, your heart catches fire and your eyes are opened.

As part of my job as a pastor, I do a lot of weddings. One of the strange side-effects of this is that I often see pictures of myself in other people's houses. Because I'm the guy who pronounces them husband and wife, the wedding photographer often catches me in the background, smiling and clapping as the married couple have their first kiss. But I know that the picture isn't really about *me*. It's about *them*, and I just happen to be there in the background. For me to think the photo was primarily about me would be the height of ignorance, or arrogance, or both.

When we read the Scriptures, Jesus is the centrepiece. He's the one the photographer was trying to capture. We're there too, in the background, and we can appreciate that and give thanks for it. But the Bible isn't about you. It's about him.

Jesus is the new Adam, who passed his garden test by submitting to the will of the Father, crushed the snake, and gave life to the dead rather than death to the living. Jesus is the new Eve, the ancestor of all new life, through whom the promised rescue finally comes about.

Jesus is the new Abel, whose blood announces that family feuds, murder and death are on the way out, and that subsequent generations will be acquitted rather than condemned. Jesus is the new Enoch, who knows God, walks with him, and is not subject to the power of the grave. Jesus is the new Noah, who finds favour in the eyes of the Lord, and in whom humans are rescued from the judgment they deserve. Jesus is the new Abraham, who trusts God, leaves his homeland to start a new nation, and ends up inheriting the world with his galaxy of descendants.

Jesus is the new Isaac, the miraculous child, offered as a sacrifice out of obedience to God

Jesus is the new Isaac, the miraculous child, offered as a sacrifice out of obedience to God, and rescued from death when all seemed lost. Jesus is the new Jacob, who saw heaven opened, received the promises, wrestled with God, and commissioned twelve guys to bless the nations. Jesus is the lion of Judah, praised by his brothers and victorious over his enemies, to whom the whole world brings tribute and obedience. Jesus is the new Joseph, the beloved son who is sold for the price of a slave, abandoned, and left for dead, but who remains faithful and then gets lifted up to the right hand of the King of the world. And that's just in Genesis.

You're not the centre of Scripture. He is.

6

Red and Black:

THE CANON OF SCRIPTURE

So far in this book, I've been using terms like 'the Scriptures' and 'the Bible' as if what I mean by it and what Jesus meant by it are the same – as if Jesus was carrying an English Bible around with him, complete with maps, and published by Hodder & Stoughton (also available in crimson bonded leather). Clearly, he wasn't. Apart from anything else, the twenty-seven books of our New Testament hadn't been written yet.

I've also been using these words as if all Christians, from that day to this, have agreed what should be included in 'the Bible'. We haven't. If you look up 'biblical canon' on Wikipedia, you'll find eight different lists of scriptural books, from all over the world, and well over one hundred different books (or parts of books) that have, at some point, been included in a 'Bible'. There are probably only sixty-six in yours.

Hmmm. What now?

Well, two things. Firstly, we should point out that the sixty-six you have are the sixty-six uncontroversial ones. The Protestant, Roman Catholic, Eastern Orthodox, Oriental Orthodox and Assyrian Bibles all have those sixty-six books – thirty-nine in the Old Testament and twenty-seven in the New – and they have all been accepted, by all branches of the Church, since the fourth century. None of the others have. So there's that.[18]

But secondly and more importantly, we look to Jesus. What did he regard as 'the Scriptures', at the time? Did he think any other words might be placed alongside it, as a result of his ministry? If so, which ones, and how would we know?

The meaning of 'the Scriptures' in Jesus' own ministry is fairly easy, because he is almost certainly talking about the twenty-four scrolls of the Hebrew Bible: the Law, the Prophets, and the Writings. (These, translated, form the thirty-nine books of our Old Testament.) On

Easter Sunday, in the evening, he appears to his disciples to explain what is happening, and says, 'This is what I told you while I was still with you: everything must be fulfilled that is written about me in the Law of Moses, the Prophets and the Psalms.'[19] He often refers to 'the Law and the Prophets', which is a common way of referring to the Hebrew Bible, and quotes it without ever quoting any of the 'apocryphal' texts. He also warns his hearers, rather grotesquely, that all the blood of the prophets 'from the blood of Abel to the blood of Zechariah' will be charged against them; since Abel and Zechariah are murdered in the first and last books of the Hebrew Bible, this is another clue.[20] Because of this, we can assume that the Scriptures, according to Jesus, included just the thirty-nine books of our Old Testament.

So far, so good. But if we stopped there, we wouldn't do justice to the way Jesus regarded his own words and actions as carrying Scripture-level authority. Consider the way he talked: 'You've heard this, but I'm saying you should do that. If you hear these words of mine and do them, you're like a smart guy who built his house on rock – but if you don't, then good luck with your sandcastle when the tsunami comes. You are my followers if you keep my commands. I haven't spoken on my own authority, but the Father told me what to say. Go and make disciples, teaching them to obey everything I've commanded you.'[21] And so on, and so on. If we closed the canon with Malachi, and left out all of Jesus' words (the red letters in some Bibles), we'd miss the whole point of what Jesus was saying and doing. That's why all Christians, everywhere, have treated the four Gospels as part of the Bible.

There's something else, too, and it's something we could easily miss: Jesus didn't think the story ended with him. In fact, when he told his followers what would happen after he had gone, he said it would be *even better* than when he was around. You'll have the Holy Spirit with you, he said, to guide you into the truth. You'll be my witnesses, everywhere. You'll teach people what I said, and you'll tell people what I've done, and you'll be sent out in the same way as I have been. Wait here, for

Jesus didn't think the story ended with him

now. But when the Spirit comes, you'll receive power. Go.

That Spirit-fuelled, resurrection-witnessing, apostolic work – the task of proclaiming Jesus, and teaching people how to live in response to the message, in rapidly changing circumstances – is what the rest of the New Testament is about. Without it, we wouldn't have much idea what the death and resurrection of Jesus actually meant; we wouldn't have the first clue how Jews and Gentiles were supposed to live together if Gentiles became part of God's family; and we wouldn't know how to preach the gospel, live the Christian life, be the church, wait for Christ's return, teach good doctrine ... it doesn't bear thinking about. And Jesus knew that. So he sent out the twelve, and his brother James, and a former Christian-hater called Paul, to teach the church under the inspiration of God's Spirit.[22] Consequently, the things they said, did and wrote are included in our understanding of 'Scripture' as well.[23]

If that seems like a lot to take in, just remember these two ideas. One: the sixty-six books you have in your Bible are all the uncontroversial ones, and all Christians everywhere accept them. Two: all the Scriptures – Old and New Testaments, red and black letters – are authoritative because of Jesus. So take up and read!

7

The Ship Is Made for the Ocean:

THE FULFILMENT OF SCRIPTURE

'Don't get the impression that I've come to get rid of the Law and the Prophets,' Jesus said. 'In fact, anyone who dumbs them down, or tells other people they're irrelevant, will be at the bottom of the pile when the kingdom comes. I haven't come to get rid of them. I've come to fulfil them.'[24]

That's a huge claim. Imagine hearing it for the first time. 'This massive, sweeping story all points to me. This multi-volume collection of laws, wise sayings, songs, stories, visions and poems finds its climax in yours truly. I've come to fulfil it all. I'm what it was all about in the first place. I'm the turning point in the movie. The headline act. The show-stopper. I'm the World Cup final. I'm Frodo and Sam casting the ring into the fiery lake. I'm the Sistine Chapel. I'm the moment you've all been waiting for, whether you know it or not.' If it wasn't Jesus speaking, it would sound ridiculous.

Fulfilment is about bringing a story to its appointed goal. When a couple say their wedding vows, they are 'fulfilling' their engagement. When a ship leaves the dock on its maiden voyage, it is 'fulfilling' its design and construction. Fulfilment doesn't mean the *end* of the story – the couple remain together; the ship remains at sea – but it means that the story continues in a different phase, because the whole point of the first part of the story has been achieved. When this happens, it doesn't mean that the first part of the story is undermined, disrespected or abolished. Far from it. The whole reason for building the ship was so that people could take her to sea. The engagement ring was always intended to sit next to a wedding ring.

This helps us make sense of something which has often puzzled readers of the Gospels. How can Jesus say things like, 'You've heard this, but I tell you *this*,' and yet still claim that he's not abolishing the Law?[25] How can he move beyond what Moses said about divorce?[26] How can he pick grain and heal people on the Sabbath, even though the Law says Jews shouldn't do any work then?[27]

When you get your head round the nature of fulfilment, though, you realise that the *purpose* of the law is being beautifully achieved in each of these examples. Moses gave commands about murder, oaths, adultery, divorce and retaliation because he was dealing with a hard-hearted nation who needed laws to protect themselves. But he also looked forward to a day when they would receive new hearts, and would obey the law in a far more radical way: no anger, lust, broken marriages or violence.[28] The Old Testament gave instructions about the Sabbath

> *The Old Testament gave instructions about the Sabbath to ensure that people rested, and trusted, in God*

to ensure that people rested, and trusted, in God – and it also pointed forward to a day when humans would experience the full Sabbath blessing of God, with all their needs provided for and all their sicknesses healed.

So when Jesus says he has come to fulfil the Law and the Prophets, he isn't being clever-clever. He's saying that the ship was always meant for the ocean, and the engagement was always pointing towards a wedding, and the Law and the Prophets were always going to climax in a new King, a new people, and a new heart. Paul, writing a quarter of a century later, summed it up beautifully: 'Christ is the culmination of the law so that there may be righteousness for everyone who believes.'[29] Indeed he is.

8

You Can Always Trust the Light:

THE CLARITY OF SCRIPTURE

Jesus knew, all too well, that lots of people who read the Scriptures did not really understand them. It's true today, and it was true in the first century. There are all sorts of issues over which modern Christians disagree – baptism, spiritual gifts, the end times, church government, and so on – and if you read church history, you'll soon discover that we're not the first generation like that. So Christians often ask: 'Is the Bible clear? Surely, if it was, we'd all agree on what it meant?'

There are two answers we could give to that question. The first is: when it comes to the essentials, we do. All Christians, everywhere, believe in one church, one Spirit, one hope, one Lord Jesus Christ, one faith, one baptism, one God.[30] Whenever I feel discouraged about the confusions and debates within the global church, I go and read the Nicene Creed, and it reminds me just how much we agree on.[31]

The second answer to that question – 'If the Bible was clear, wouldn't we all agree about everything?' – is: not necessarily. There are all sorts of things our end – ignorance, hard-heartedness, sin, rebellion, unbelief – which might prevent us from understanding what Scripture says quite clearly. In fact, when Jesus interacted with people who had misunderstood something he'd said, either in Scripture or in person, he *never* put the blame on the word of God for being unclear, confusing or obscure. Instead, he *always* said it was something to do with the readers or hearers:

> 'Are you also still without understanding?'[32]

> 'You make void the word of God by your tradition that you've handed down.'[33]

'Do you still not perceive? How is it that you fail to understand that I wasn't talking about bread?'[34]

'This people's heart has grown dull, and with their ears they can barely hear, and their eyes they have closed.'[35]

'O foolish ones, and slow of heart to believe all that the prophets have spoken! Wasn't it necessary that the Christ should suffer these things, and enter into his glory?'[36]

'Get behind me, Satan! You are a hindrance to me.'[37]

'But they didn't understand this saying, and it was concealed from them, so that they might not perceive it. And they were afraid to ask him about it.'[38]

'Why do you not understand what I say? It is because you cannot bear to hear my word.'[39]

'It is the Scriptures that bear witness about me, yet you refuse to come to me that you may have life.'[40]

Ignorance. Traditionalism. Naivety. Dullness. Deafness. Foolishness. Opposition to God. Fear. Sin. Stubbornness. When people don't understand something God has said, Jesus assumes that the Scriptures are clear – 'Haven't you read in the Scriptures?!' – and the people are muddled. Frequently, in our arrogance, we assume it's the other way round.

It's easy to see how, in all sorts of situations, misunderstandings could be our responsibility. I might disagree with you about baptism because I'm stubborn, and mired in my tradition. I might disagree with you about the end times because I'm ignorant, or proud, or naive. I might disagree with you about spiritual gifts out of fear, or hard-heartedness. (Of course, we might also disagree about something because Scripture doesn't speak clearly about our particular questions. It doesn't tell us who to vote for, whether to drink tea, or how to structure our corporate worship, for instance.) But whatever the reason, we can all agree on this: the problem is probably at our end, rather than God's end.

I teach on several theology courses, and I always make a point of telling my students that a number of the things I'll teach them will be untrue. I never intend to teach wrongly, of course, and I work hard to ensure my teaching is as accurate and helpful as possible, but the reality is that I will teach some things that are incorrect. When that happens, though, I don't want anyone to think it's because the Bible isn't clear where it intends to be. It may be that the Bible wasn't intended to address the particular question I'm asking, or it may be that I've been waylaid by some combination of ignorance, carelessness and sin. It certainly won't be because the Scriptures are an incoherent mess.

'Your word is a lamp for my feet,' wrote the Psalmist, 'a light on my path.'[41] When you're walking along a dark and narrow track, you can't always trust your judgment. But you can always trust the light.

9

Judgment, Miracles, Sex and Stuff:

THE CHALLENGES OF SCRIPTURE

Let's be honest: the Scriptures can be difficult.

Sometimes, as we have already seen, the difficulties come from within the texts themselves.[42] Accounts vary, theology develops, tensions exist and authors bring different perspectives on things (not to mention the fact that all the texts were written in languages and cultures which are completely different from ours).

In my experience, though, most of these difficulties are fairly easy to resolve, with a mixture of study, imagination and honesty. They can make people puzzled, but they rarely make people angry. The things that really get people riled up, at least in our day, are areas where Scripture challenges our deeply held beliefs (or where Scripture is challenged by them, depending on which way you look at it). When you get into conversations about the Bible, you find that the biggest challenges for most people are not over issues where the Bible is unclear, but over issues where the Bible is very clear, and people don't like it. Judgment. Miracles. Sex. Things like that.

As part of my job, I often end up debating with people about the Bible. Some of them are very troubled by the idea of miracles, especially the very dramatic ones: parting the Red Sea, making shadows go backwards, raising the dead, and so on. Others love the miracles, but object strongly to the idea that God ever kills people as an act of judgment, either directly (like raining down fire from heaven) or indirectly (using humans or angels

Others ... have looked to 'update' what the Bible says about sex and sexuality

to do it). Others, particularly in the last couple of decades, have increasingly looked to 'update' what the Bible says about sex and sexuality, to make it fit more closely with the preferences of modern people. When faced with these sorts of challenges, what is the best approach?

The answer, as ever, is to look at Jesus. In a general sense, we can obviously look to Jesus' view of the Bible, as we've been doing throughout this book: if Scripture teaches it, then our loving Father wants us to believe it and obey it, for his glory and for our good. But specifically, we can also look to the things Jesus says about each of these issues. When we do that, we find that his teaching is – as we would expect! – uncompromising, and yet loving.

With miracles, things are obvious. You can't read the Jesus story without tripping over miracles on every page, both in what he says, and in what he does: healing, feeding, storm-calming, resurrecting, and the rest. All the historical evidence we have shows that Jesus was known as a miracle-worker, and the only way you can get rid of that conclusion is to go through the Gospels with scissors, and cut them all out. (This, in a wonderful parody of modern liberalism, is exactly what President Thomas Jefferson did. He wasn't left with much, as you can imagine.) Writing a history of Jesus without any miracles would be like writing a history of Churchill without any wars.

Or take judgment. Many of us find it hard to imagine Jesus, the meek and mild mellow-man, approving of some of the fierce divine judgment that happens in the Old Testament: cataclysmic floods wiping everyone out, the destruction of entire cities, and so on. Yet in teaching his disciples, he not only affirms that all of these things happened – Noah's flood, fire and sulphur raining down from heaven on Sodom, plus Lot's wife being turned into a pillar of salt – but he also uses them as ways of describing what his own coming will be like.[43] 'God sometimes kills people in judgment,' he says, 'and when he does, it happens suddenly, and it catches people out. Well: the same will be true when the Son of Man comes. So make sure you're ready.'

Or how about sex? Occasionally you hear it said, in a slightly Thomas Jefferson-ish way, that Jesus had nothing to say about sex (which is usually supposed to imply that we can pretty much do what we like). What a lot of cobblers. Right near the start of his most famous sermon, he talked about adultery, lust, divorce, remarriage and sexual immorality.[44] When describing what makes people unclean, he gave adultery and sexual immorality as prominent examples.[45] More importantly, when teaching on marriage, he went back to the garden story – one man, one woman, marriage, sex, permanence – as the foundation for all subsequent teaching.[46] And he affirmed the dignity and beauty of singleness, not only in principle (by talking about it) but in practice (by living it).[47] For all of us living in

Whenever Scripture challenges some of our deeply held beliefs, we have a choice

a sex-saturated world, the fact that we follow a single guy, who never had sex and yet lived the most full life there is, should be a huge encouragement.

The point is: whenever Scripture challenges some of our deeply held beliefs, as it often does, we have a choice. We can challenge the Bible, or we can let the Bible challenge us. We can do a Jefferson on it, cutting out the bits we like and binning the rest. Or we can do a Jesus on it, affirming the accuracy of the Bible in spite of the difficulties we have with it, and allow it to refine our view of God, the world, sexuality, or whatever it may be. Personally, I'd go with Jesus on that one.

10

Oh No, They Won't:

THE SUFFICIENCY OF SCRIPTURE

The parables of Jesus often have cryptic, subversive and even menacing punchlines. The lovely story about the runaway son and his homecoming party ends with a sour-faced older brother shaming his dad and refusing to come in.[48] The wedding feast is open to everyone, rich and poor and everyone in between, except the gatecrasher who comes in wearing the wrong clothes.[49] The easy-geezer wheeler-dealer manager is commended for ripping off his boss, and held up as an example for us.[50] We could go on.

One of the darkest punchlines of all comes at the end of the story about the rich man and Lazarus.[51] It looks like a simple story of role reversal: the poor man dies and goes to be with Abraham, and the rich man dies and ends up in torment. But it ends with a strange piece of dialogue between the rich man, pleading for help, and Abraham. 'Send Lazarus to my father's house,' the rich man cries, 'so they don't end up here!' Abraham says no – they can all read Moses and the Prophets for themselves. 'No, that won't be enough!' pleads the rich man. 'If someone rises from the dead, though, they'll repent. Please, Abraham. Please.' But Abraham, again, says no. If they don't listen to Moses and the Prophets, then nobody rising from the dead will convince them.

The story, like many of Jesus' stories, is about wealth, poverty and the great reversals of the kingdom. But the punchline looks for all the world like it's about the sufficiency of Scripture. Roughly translated, Abraham is saying: if people want to know how to be saved, they can read the Law and the Prophets, and they'll repent. But if they don't, then not even a resurrection will persuade them. The Scriptures are enough.

In our world, there are countless people who agree with the rich man on this one. I was at primary school when I first heard someone say they'd believe the gospel if God would only perform a one-off miracle in front of them. Twenty-five years later, I heard an atheist on the radio say the same thing. Weirdly, miracles done in front of other people, or in other generations, don't count. *I'm an individual, entitled to my own opinions,* they think, *so if God wants me to believe, he's going to have to do a special miracle, just for me. Then, and only then, I'll believe.*

And Abraham says, 'Oh no, you won't.'

Scripture, you see, is sufficient. It's enough. It reveals who God is, and who we are, and what God has done about it, and what we need to do about it. We don't need extra miracles to reveal the gospel. We don't need extra revelations.[52] We can read the Scriptures – and if we don't believe them, then no amount of party-piece sky-writing will work.

We need to hear that truth in the church, as well. We don't need visions to believe that heaven is for real; we know it from the Scriptures, and especially through Jesus. We don't need miracles to confirm that God loves us; we know it from the Scriptures, and especially through Jesus.

We don't need great wealth, or freedom from suffering, to tell us that God is for us; we know it from the Scriptures, and especially through Jesus. As Paul was later to write, Scripture has been inspired by God, so that we 'may be *thoroughly* equipped for *every* good work'.[53]

In other words, assuming we pay attention to what it says, the Bible is enough.

11

Restless Idol-Factories:

THE DANGER OF SCRIPTURE

'You carefully rummage through the Scriptures,' says Jesus to the Judeans, 'because you think that you get eternal life from them. But they all point to me – and yet you refuse to come to me, and get life.'[54]

Every gift is potentially dangerous. We have this endless capacity, as humans, to worship gifts rather than the gift-Giver: food, sex, the sun, prosperity, knowledge, art. Perhaps surprisingly, and worryingly, the same is true of Scripture. Because the Bible is God's word to us, and because of its beauty and power and richness and depth, it is possible to think that it is the

Bible which gives life, rather than Jesus. It is possible for our hearts, restless idol-factories that they are, to take one of God's greatest gifts and accidentally make a god out of it.

Sometimes this can be for emotional reasons, and can seem rather trivial. A friend of mine once told me that she used to hug her Bible, as a substitute for God, because she so struggled with the fact that God wasn't physical. I doubt that's the end of the world, although it probably isn't a coincidence that she came from a church where sharing bread and wine together – which is the physical way Jesus told us to experience him – was rare.

Sometimes it can be for intellectual reasons, and rather more serious. Some of us, as a result of our personalities and backgrounds, can find the Scriptures easier to manage than the Holy Spirit. We know that, if we study hard, apply our minds, read lots and reason carefully, we can grasp the Bible well; the Holy Spirit, on the other hand, is a person with whom we are called to relationship, and our brainpower doesn't always guarantee intimacy. For the academically minded, there is a fairly well-established path to success with the Bible: a degree, a Master's, a doctorate, published works, and so on; keeping in step with the Spirit doesn't work that way. The result is that the Scriptures can, oh-so-subtly, take the place of God, and we can end up with a functional Trinity of Father, Son and Holy Bible. 'The Bible will guide you into all truth,' we imagine Jesus saying in John 16. 'It is good for you that I'm going away, because if I don't, the Bible won't come to you.' I'm joking, of course. But only just.[55]

Sometimes it can be for spiritual reasons, and these are the most dangerous of all. Jesus tells the Judeans that they *refused* to come to him and have life, even though the Scriptures testified about him. They knew about the Messiah from the Bible, yet they didn't *want* the life he was offering, because of what it would cost them. Without knowing it, they

> **Jesus tells the Judeans that they refused to come to him and have life, even though the Scriptures testified about him**

had put the Scriptures in the place that only God should be, with the result that they failed to recognise God when he was, quite literally, staring them in the face. Hugging Bibles is unnecessary, and intellectualising Christianity is unhelpful. But rejecting Jesus because of our beliefs about the Bible is hellish, not to mention the most tragic case of missing the wood for the trees.

Bibliolatry – the worship of the Bible – is not the main problem in our day. Most people's view of the Bible is too low, rather than too high. But as with any good gift, there is the danger of idolatry. The Scriptures are there to point to God: Father, Son and Holy Spirit. We most honour them when we find our life, and our joy, in him.

Epilogue:

THE INTERPRETATION OF SCRIPTURE

This book is very short – deliberately – so there's obviously a huge amount of material we haven't covered. In particular, we haven't really looked at how we interpret Scripture, except to say that we interpret it in light of Jesus. Many people today, for example, cannot understand why Christians obey some instructions in the Bible but not others: why we seek to love God, love our neighbours, preach the gospel, only have sex within marriage and gather in local churches, while not feeling the need to abstain from shellfish, circumcise boys, stone adulterers, wear head coverings in church (if we're women), kiss each other (if we're men), rip our eyes out if we sin, avoid black pudding, and take trips to Troas to find Paul's coat.

So here are five interpretive principles which will hopefully help you navigate some of these questions:

When interpreted correctly, with careful attention paid to context, purpose, genre and authorial intention, the Scriptures do not contain mistakes. (We've talked about this in the book already.)

The primary way of establishing the meaning of a text is to establish what the original author meant their original audience to understand. (This is the golden rule of interpretation, in my view, and it helps us avoid all sorts of weird and wonderful interpretations. Nobody listening to Jesus thought we were *literally* supposed to rip our eyes out, for example.[56])

The Bible is a big story, and the big story is authoritative for all Christians, although instructions given in one part of the story are not necessarily binding on those who live in other parts of the story. (The law of Moses, for example, was given to ancient Israel, who lived before the coming of Jesus – the 'destination of the law'. That means that the instructions we find there are fulfilled and summed up in the commands to love God and love our neighbour, rather than needing to be followed to the letter by all subsequent Christians. The early church were careful to explain, for instance, that all foods were clean, that Gentiles didn't have to circumcise their baby boys, and so on, because the law had been fulfilled in Jesus.[57])

We live in the same part of the story as the New Testament church, and therefore we should obey all instructions given to believers in the New Testament, unless there are clear indications that they only apply to specific individuals. (Occasionally, there are. Only Timothy was supposed to go to Troas to find Paul's coat; only the Romans were supposed to greet the household of Aristobulus; only those with an emperor are supposed to honour the emperor; and so on.[58])

> *We live in the same part of the story as the New Testament church*

Obeying New Testament instructions will sometimes require cultural translation, where the meaning of symbols has changed across the centuries, in order to preserve the meaning of the original symbols. (Men kissing men, for example, is a physical symbol that means something different in the UK to what it meant in the Mediterranean in the first century. The same is true of head coverings for men and women, footwashing, and a handful of other things. To obey these instructions requires 'translating' the symbols, if you like.[59])

These five principles won't resolve every question, sadly – people will still disagree about what the original author meant (principle 2) and what 'clear indications' are (principle 4) – but they'll resolve an awful lot of them. Plus, they'll give you a decent response to the 'Why do Christians fight slavery but not stone people?' type of questions.

Further Reading

Finally, here are a few books which may help you go further in your understanding of what the Bible is, and how best to understand it.

Kevin DeYoung, *Taking God at His Word* (IVP, 2014).
A simple but robust explanation of the doctrine of Scripture, from a conservative evangelical point of view.

Tom Wright, *Scripture and the Authority of God* (SPCK, revised edition 2013).
An insightful study of how the authority of God in Scripture actually works, from one of the world's leading Christian scholars.

J. Scott Duvall and **J. Daniel Hays**, *Grasping God's Word* (Zondervan, third edition 2012).
A textbook on hermeneutics, complete with clear principles, illustrations, exercises and study guides.

Gordon D. Fee and **Douglas Stuart**, *How to Read the Bible For All It's Worth* (Zondervan, fourth edition 2014).
A shorter and simpler introduction to hermeneutics from two evangelical scholars.

Kevin J. Vanhoozer, *The Drama of Doctrine* (Westminster John Knox Press, 2004).
A much more substantial volume from a leading evangelical theologian, which focuses on how the biblical story shapes our theology.

Endnotes

Introduction: Where do we start?

1   If you're wondering how anyone could trust
     in Jesus without first believing the Bible is
     all true, either read my little book *If God
     Then What?*, or ask any global Christian
     who doesn't even own a Bible. You might
     be surprised.

2   Some would argue that we cannot know
     what Jesus was like, and how he spoke and
     acted, unless we assume the Bible is infallible
     first. But this is not the case. We have
     four ancient documents, the four Gospels
     (which record eyewitness testimony of
     what Jesus said about the Scriptures), as well
     as dozens of early Christian texts (which
     reveal a similar commit-ment to scriptural

authority), and numerous other Jewish sources (which indicate that Jesus, as a Jew, would likely have had a high regard for the Law, the Prophets and the Writings). Given the contro-versies that happened in the first few decades of the church, over scriptural matters like circumcision, food laws and so on, we can be confident that if Jesus had criticised the Hebrew Bible or implied that it was wrong in some way, we would know about it.

1. The Art Of War: The Authority Of Scripture

3   Genesis 3:1.

4   You can read about this in Matthew 4:1–11. My account is paraphrased.

5   See Deuteronomy 6:16.

2. True Like Jazz: The Inspiration Of Scripture

6   This story is in Matthew 22:41–46 and Mark 12:35–37, but is paraphrased here.

7   2 Peter 1:21.

8   2 Timothy 3:16.

3. Dodging The Rocks: The Unbreakability Of Scripture

9   This story appears in John 10:22–39, but is paraphrased here.

10   It's common to hear people say things like, 'The Scriptures aren't the word of God; Jesus is the Word of God.' This comment from Jesus – referring to the Scriptures as the word of God – debunks that way of thinking.

11   Matthew 5:17–19.

4. One Bride For Seven Brothers: The Coherence Of Scripture

12   See Mark 12:18–27. My account is paraphrased.

13   Exodus 3.

14   We could give lots of examples, but probably the clearest one is Proverbs 26:4–5, where two directly opposing statements are put next to each other. Should you answer a fool according to his folly, or not? The answer is: yes and no.

15 For my money, this is the best response to the puzzle over the two differing genealogies of Jesus (in Matthew 1 and Luke 3), although plenty of solutions have been suggested: we just don't know enough to figure out exactly how to hold them together. And that's OK.

16 For example: how did Judas die? Matthew 27:3–10 says he hanged himself; Acts 1:18–19 says he fell headlong and burst open in the middle. The authors are emphasising different aspects of a notorious event, but the two accounts can easily be harmonised with a bit of (slightly gruesome) imagination. Similarly, the four resurrection accounts (Matthew 28; Mark 16; Luke 24; John 20) require a mixture of patience, imagination and guesswork to fit together into one story (although we should always be careful not to 'flatten' the stories into one account – all four narrators bring different emphases, and we need to make sure we respect them!). A superb resource which analyses 101 alleged contradictions in the Bible, and is free online, can be found at http://www.debate.org.uk/debate-topics/apologetic/contrads/.

5. It's Not About You: The Centre Of Scripture

17   Luke 24:13–35, paraphrased.

6. Red And Black: The Canon Of Scripture

18   These are sometimes called the 'protocanonical' books, as opposed to the 'deuterocanonical' ones. Of the fifty-two others, half are now excluded from the primary canon by all branches of Christianity. The remaining twenty-six are all prophetic, historical or wisdom writings which emerged after the end of the Old Testament; some parts of the church accept them, and others do not. The most significant ten of these – seven books (Tobit, Judith, 1&2 Maccabees, Wisdom, Sirach and Baruch) and three fragments of other books (Esther, Baruch and Daniel) – form what is sometimes called the 'Apocrypha', and appear in some English translations of the Bible today.

19   Luke 24:44. This probably refers to the three sections of the Hebrew Bible: the

Law *(Torah)*, the Prophets *(Nevi'im)* and the Writings *(Ketuvim)*, which collectively are abbreviated to TaNaKh.

20　Luke 11:50–51.

21　Matthew 5:21–48; 7:24–27; John 15:14; 12:49; Matthew 28:19–20. I have paraphrased Jesus' words.

22　Paul, like the twelve, receives a direct commission from Jesus, as well as a resurrection appearance of him (Acts 9:1–19; 22:1–21; 26:12–23; 1 Corinthians 15:8–9; Galatians 1:11–24). When he is teaching churches, he is fairly clear that he is inspired by God (see for example 1 Corinthians 7:40; 14:36–38).

23　The New Testament, then, comprises the things Jesus said and did (Matthew to John), the things his witnesses said and did (Acts), and the letters written by some of his witnesses: Paul, James, Peter and John. The exceptions are Hebrews (which is anonymous, but was soon recognised as carrying apostolic authority), and Jude (who may or may not be the brother of Jesus).

For a proper explanation of the canon, see Michael J. Kruger's book, *Canon Revisited* (Crossway, 2012).

7. The Ship Is Made For The Ocean: The Fulfilment Of Scripture

24 Matthew 5:17–20, paraphrased.

25 Matthew 5:21, 27, 31, 33, 38 compared to Matthew 5:22, 28, 32, 34, 39.

26 Matthew 19:1–12.

27 Luke 6:1–11.

28 Deuteronomy 30:6–10.

29 Romans 10:4. The word *telos*, often translated 'end' here, has both the idea of 'finish' and 'purpose', like our modern English word 'destination'.

8. You Can Always Trust The Light: The Clarity Of Scripture

30 Ephesians 4:4–6.

31 The Nicene Creed states, 'We believe in one God, the Father, the Almighty, maker of heaven and earth, of all that is, seen

and unseen. We believe in one Lord, Jesus Christ, the only son of God, eternally begotten of the Father, God from God, Light from Light, true God from true God, begotten, not made, of one being with the Father. Through him all things were made. For us and for our salvation he came down from heaven: by the power of the Holy Spirit he became incarnate from the Virgin Mary, and was made man. For our sake he was crucified under Pontius Pilate; he suffered death and was buried. On the third day he rose again in accordance with the Scriptures; he ascended into heaven and is seated at the right hand of the Father. He will come again in glory to judge the living and the dead, and his kingdom will have no end. We believe in the Holy Spirit, the Lord, the giver of life, who proceeds from the Father [and the Son]. With the Father and the Son he is worshipped and glorified. He has spoken through the Prophets. We believe in one holy catholic and apostolic Church. We acknowledge one baptism for the forgiveness of sins. We look for the resurrection of the dead, and the life of the world to come.'

32   Matthew 15:16, paraphrased.

33   Mark 7:13, paraphrased.

34   Matthew 16:9–11, paraphrased.

35   Matthew 13:15, paraphrased.

36   Luke 24:25–26, paraphrased.

37   Matthew 16:23, paraphrased.

38   Luke 9:45, paraphrased.

39   John 8:43, paraphrased.

40   John 5:39–40, paraphrased.

41   Psalm 119:105.

9. Judgment, Miracles, Sex And Stuff: The Challenges Of Scripture

42   See chapter 4 both for some examples of these difficulties and for some help in resolving them.

43   Luke 17:22–37.

44   Matthew 5:27–32. The Greek word porneia here is a catch-all word for sexual activity

that is off-limits in the Law – effectively, sex outside of marriage.

45 Matthew 15:19–20; Mark 7:21–23.

46 Matthew 19:1–12; Mark 10:1–12.

47 See Matthew 19:12, where those who 'choose to live like eunuchs for the sake of the kingdom of heaven' are probably those who, like Jesus, John the Baptist and Paul, have remained single.

10. Oh No, They Won't:
The Sufficiency Of Scripture

48 Luke 15:11–32.

49 Matthew 22:1–14.

50 Luke 16:1–9.

51 Luke 16:19–31, paraphrased.

52 I don't say any of this to denigrate miracles, prophetic revelation, or anything else (and I myself have frequently seen and experienced both). Jesus wasn't saying that these things weren't valuable, or God-given; when he told this parable, he hadn't yet risen from

the dead himself! He was simply saying that they aren't necessary to save, because the Law and the Prophets are enough.

53   2 Timothy 3:16–17, italics my emphasis.

11. Restless Idol-Factories:
The Danger Of Scripture

54   John 5:39–40, paraphrased.

55   There is a great chapter on this whole idea, called 'Confessions of a Bible Deist', in Jack Deere's book *Surprised by the Voice of God* (Kingsway, 2006).

Epilogue: The Interpretation Of Scripture

56   Matthew 5:29.

57   Mark 7:19; Romans 14:14; Galatians 5:6.

58   2 Timothy 4:13; Romans 16:10; 1 Peter 2:13–17.

59   2 Corinthians 13:12; 1 Corinthians 11:2–16; John 13:14–15.

Union

We fuel reformation in churches and lives.

Union Publishing invests in the next generation of leaders with theology that gives them a taste for a deeper knowledge of God. From books to our free online content, we are committed to producing excellent resources that will refresh, transform, and grow believers and their churches.

We want people everywhere to know, love, and enjoy God, glorifying him in everything they do. For this reason, we've collected hundreds of free articles, podcasts, book chapters, and video content for our free online collection. We also produce a fresh stream of written, audio, and video resources to help you to be more fully alive in the truth, goodness, and beauty of Jesus.

If you are hungry for reformational resources that will help you delight in God and grow in Christ, we'd love for you to visit us at unionpublishing.org.

unionpublishing.org